CHRISTMAS CAROLS
FOR TROMBONE

HAL•LEONARD
Easy INSTRUMENTAL PLAY-ALONG

Audio Access Included

T0081325

CONTENTS

2 **Angels We Have Heard on High**

2 **Christ Was Born on Christmas Day**

3 **Come, All Ye Shepherds**

4 **Come, Thou Long-Expected Jesus**

5 **Good Christian Men, Rejoice**

6 **Jingle Bells**

8 **Jolly Old St. Nicholas**

8 **Lo, How a Rose E'er Blooming**

6 **On Christmas Night**

7 **Up on the Housetop**

To access audio visit:
www.halleonard.com/mylibrary

Enter Code
6211-8265-9109-5571

Audio Arrangements by Peter Deneff
Tracking, mixing, and mastering by BeatHouse Music

ISBN 978-1-4803-9606-7

HAL•LEONARD®
CORPORATION

7777 W. BLUEMOUND RD. P.O. BOX 13819 MILWAUKEE, WI 53213

In Australia Contact:
Hal Leonard Australia Pty. Ltd.
4 Lentara Court
Cheltenham, Victoria, 3192 Australia
Email: ausadmin@halleonard.com.au

Visit Hal Leonard Online at
www.halleonard.com

ANGELS WE HAVE HEARD ON HIGH

Traditional French Carol

CHRIST WAS BORN ON CHRISTMAS DAY

Traditional

Play 3 times

COME, ALL YE SHEPHERDS

Traditional Czech Text
Traditional Moravian Melody

COME, THOU LONG-EXPECTED JESUS

Words by CHARLES WESLEY
Music by ROWLAND HUGH PRICHARD

GOOD CHRISTIAN MEN, REJOICE

14th Century Latin Text
14th Century German Melody

JINGLE BELLS

Words and Music by
J. PIERPONT

ON CHRISTMAS NIGHT

Sussex Carol

UP ON THE HOUSETOP

Words and Music by
B.R. HANBY

JOLLY OLD ST. NICHOLAS

Traditional 19th Century American Carol

LO, HOW A ROSE E'ER BLOOMING

15th Century German Carol